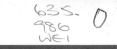
Success with

Hanging Baskets
and
Trailing Plants

MARTIN WEIMAR

Series Editor:
LESLEY YOUNG

MEREHURST

Foreword

Contents

Many people love the idea of a hanging garden on their balcony or patio and it is not at all difficult to design and create an overhead display of flowers and scented herbs in a favourite corner or above a garden seat. In this useful guide, Martin Weimar shows you how to transform your balcony or patio with the help of hanging baskets, boxes and other interesting plant containers.

There is a host of practical tips on securing the containers and on ways of grouping plants in them, as well as advice on the right way to water your plants and on overwintering them. Full-colour step-by-step illustrations show the correct way to do all that is necessary to create a lovely, year-round display. The section on design suggests attractive ways of grouping plants and the instructions given are easy for a novice gardener to follow. The book is divided into sections on sun-loving, semi-shade-loving and shade-loving plants to enable the reader to choose the right plants for each site.

The herbs in this basket smell delicious in the sunshine.

Petunias.

Busy Lizzies.

The author
Martin Weimar is a gardener and flower artist who has contributed to numerous art exhibitions. For many years he has given courses on designing with plants and has written several successful guides on this subject.

The photographer
Jürgen Stork has worked as a freelance photographer since 1982, mainly in the areas of fashion, advertising and nature. He has contributed photographs to many periodicals and to many of the titles in the Merehurst "Success with" gardening series.

The illustrator
Renate Holzner lives in Regensburg and works as a freelance illustrator and graphic designer. Her wide range extends from line drawings to photo-realistic computer graphics. Among her regular clients are many well-known publishing companies.

NB: Please read the Author's note on page 60 in order that your enjoyment of hanging baskets and trailing plants may not be spoiled.

Hanging flowers

There is no reason why flowering plants should remain firmly rooted in the ground. With a little help from you your plants can conquer the heights on airy balconies and patios.

Photo above: Busy Lizzies are decorative in shady places.
Photo left: Rudbeckia, lobelia, ivy and busy Lizzie waiting to be planted in baskets.

Hanging flowers

Cascades of flowers on different levels

Many people would love to accommodate more and more plants on a balcony or patio that is already packed with luxuriant greenery but are not sure where to fit them in. Do not despair: there is more room – above your head – and this guide will show you a multitude of possibilities for adding to your plant collection. You can design attractive arrangements in hanging baskets or even plant them in your own individually designed plant containers. If you choose the right plants and care for them properly, your overhead garden will turn into a feast for the eye and can even provide food for the table.

The Hanging Gardens of Babylon

One of the seven wonders of the ancient world was the legendary garden that Semiramis, Queen of Babylon, is supposed to have created some 3,000 years ago. She built the famous Hanging Gardens of Babylon, so the story goes, to remind her of the beautiful mountainous area that she came from. The gardens were built on a slope, in many step-like terraces, one above the other.
You could design a hanging garden of your own on a balcony or patio, for example with a plant stair (photo, right) or by using a table covered in flowering plants (see p. 43).

Beauty for every season

Annual plants are ideal for planting in a hanging garden. During the course of a single year, these plants will grow and flourish and will often bloom continuously throughout a whole season. In addition, with annuals, the trouble of overwintering is avoided. Each season different plants groupings can be put together to take full advantage of their flowering times.
Spring flowers, like pansies, forget-me-nots, primroses or wallflowers, are ideal for an early, frost-hardy arrangement.
Summer flowers, like pelargoniums, petunias or lobelia can be planted after the last cold snap of late spring. They make an attractive eye-catching feature during the summer months. Once autumn arrives, they can be removed or, depending on the type of plant, overwintered in frost-free conditions (for overwintering, see p. 56).
Autumn plants like *Erica*, chrysanthemums or asters will cope with a few degrees of frost. Many spring-flowering plants are offered for sale as early as the previous autumn. With the correct care during the winter (see p. 56), they will remain hardy and present a continuous display from autumn until late spring.

Perennial planting

A hanging garden of perennials can be maintained for many years. This will, of course, require a certain amount of attention to correct care and overwintering (see p. 56). Many hardy perennials (see plant list, p. 40) will flower for only a short while but will continue to look good for the rest of the time because of their attractive green foliage.

Planning ahead

You will be able to enjoy your planting arrangements without any real problems if you consider some important points before you begin.
● Observe the light and climatic conditions at the chosen site and choose plants that will thrive in these conditions.
● Use suitable containers and make sure they are adequately secured (see pp. 10-17).
● When placing containers in certain positions, think of plant care and access etc. (see pp. 44-57). Plants that are difficult to reach generally end up being given less care.
● Make sure nothing is dangling down in your way or hinders access to areas used often, for example a seat. Always hang the

A flowering staircase.

Fruit and vegetables ready to pick.

containers in such a way that you will be unable to injure yourself on them and so that neither the plants nor your furniture can get damaged.

● Choose plants with the most suitable shapes of growth for the intended position.

● When securing heavy containers in their position, think about weight distribution and any legal responsibility you may have (see p. 15).

Designing with plants

You can increase the effect of individual plants if you remember a few rules of good design when combining them (see design ideas, pp. 20-43). A clever selection and the arrangement of plants according to their shapes of growth are particularly important points when planting a hanging garden.

Shapes of growth

You can grow plants so that cascades of flowers and foliage burst out of the containers. Look for plants with very different shapes of growth.

● Creeping or rhizome-forming plants like convolvulous (*Convolvulus sabatius*), *Scaevola*, ground ivy (*Glechoma hederacea*), strawberry plants, *Chlorophytum comosum* and ivy are ideal for making decorative hanging curtains.

● Plants that grow in the shape of large cushions, like *Portulaca*, *Dorotheanthus bellidiformis* and *Gazania* (see p. 23) work best if they are planted close to the edge of the container. Here they will form an attractive link between the plants that grow upwards and those that hang downwards.

● Plants that are bushy and pendulous, for example hanging fuchsias, hanging pelargoniums or hanging begonias, will send a wealth of blooms upwards as well as downwards (see p. 38).

● Some climbing and trailing plants, such as *Rhodochiton atrosanguineus* or nasturtium, will not require climbing aids and will grow easily over the middle and upper sections of an arrangement (see p. 32).

● Plants with upright growth, like kitchen herbs (see p. 24), are ideal for the upper level.

Planting for the best display

The level at which plants are to be grown will also determine your choice of shape and attitude of growth.

Hanging containers *at eye-level* look very effective with a combination of different shapes of growth. The upper, middle and lower parts of the planting will all be easy to see.

Plants placed *below eye-level* look best with upright, cushion-forming and bushy, overhanging plants. However, only the upperparts of the plants and those hanging over the edge of the container will be visible to the onlooker.

Containers placed *above eye-level* do not require any plants that send their flowers upwards. Here, all shapes of growth can be used provided they look decorative from below.

Balcony railings, bannisters, plant tables and plant stairs can all be equipped with different shapes of growth depending on the local conditions and climate.

Hanging flowers

Buying plants

Nurseries, garden centres and markets offer a wide selection of seasonal plants as well as ready-to-plant, flowering young plants. Your decision will depend not only on the price – young plants are cheaper – but also on the way you intend to plant them (see pp. 12/13). Vegetables are obtainable as young plants only. Growing your own plants from seed is recommended if you wish to cultivate rarities (see planting night-scented plants, p. 62) in your hanging garden and they are not available as seedlings. A few seed mail-order firms offer special seed mixtures for hanging gardens (see p. 60).

The right soil

You can use the same pre-fertilized plant compost for hanging containers that you would for balcony boxes and can obtain the various different types of compost in the trade. Garden soil is too heavy for use in containers and has a tendency to become compacted very easily. A good, light soil with a high capacity for storing water can be obtained by mixing three parts of garden soil with three parts of well-rotted, sieved garden compost and two parts each of peat or sand. Alternatively, mix garden soil and bought flower compost in a ratio of 1:1.

Positioning the plants

Depending on the site and conditions (see p. 36), you can arrange plants to one side to make a splendid show, or in the round. The gardening trade offers a wide range of containers for variations on both of these basic concepts.

Hanging baskets

One of the most ideal containers for planting an attractive all-round arrangement is a large-mesh, stable basket made of painted wire, with chains for hanging it up. Such planting containers have been used very successfully for years in many countries. A profusion of flowers pours from every opening, as both the walls and the bottom of the basket are planted through. Nowadays these baskets can be obtained almost anywhere in a range of sizes and colours, semi-spherical or with a flattened bottom. Planting them successfully requires a little skill, however (see pp. 12/13).
Alternative: If you do not own a ready-made basket, you can use a large-mesh bicycle basket made of painted wire or something similar (see photo, p. 42).
Accessories: Wire baskets require strong, ornamental hooks or brackets (see p. 13) for securing them to a house wall. These baskets can also be obtained in the form of semi-spherical bowls for securing to a wall.

Chains, wires and ropes

Builders' yards, ironmongers, rope makers and ship's chandlers can all provide useful supports for securing hanging plants.
Chains can be found in various sizes. They are distinguished by their type and capacity for carrying weight. Circular steel-link chains are very strong and are suitable for securing heavyweight plant containers. Ornamental chains are only suitable for very light containers.

My tip: The best plan is to have chains cut to the right length at the retailers.

Petunias in brilliant colours. These classic balcony flowers are always charming.

Thick chain links, in particular, cannot be cut or taken apart without using bolt cutters or a hacksaw.

Wire can be obtained on a roll in various thicknesses. Galvanized or green plastic-coated tying wire is particularly suitable. Tying wire of the sort used for making garlands or wreaths is too weak.

Galvanized wire ropes are obtainable in different gauges. They are distinguished by their weight-carrying capacity. They will need to be equipped with rope clamps (see p. 17) for hanging them up. They can be cut with sharp pliers or wire cutters.

Warning: The ends of lengths of cut wire are sharp and can cause injuries.

Plastic-coated ropes and straps are also suitable for hanging up containers. Fixing and securing them is relatively uncomplicated and they are very strong and durable. They are also obtainable in bright colours to give a plant arrangement that extra something.

Planting baskets

If you look around any garden centre or residential street you will be amazed by the luxuriantly flowering hanging baskets used for decorating balconies and patios. You can easily make your own beautiful hanging baskets if you follow a few rules.

Equipment

The following accessories are required:
a basket with a chain (see p. 10);
inserts to keep the compost in the basket and cover the lining (see below). Traditionally, sphagnum moss was used but moss from your own lawn or loose coconut fibre matting from a florist or garden centre is better for ecological reasons. Cardboard, textile or foam inserts can be obtained from the gardening trade. Some of these are biodegradable,
recyclable products.
NB: Loose lining material is not a substitute for compost. You should use lining material of the correct thickness for lining the walls of the basket so that your plants have as much compost as possible to hold nutrients and water;
polythene to keep moisture in and prevent water from running out unhindered;
plants – for a basket with a diameter of 35 cm (14 in), depending on the size of the plants, about 10-15 plants depending on how large they grow and their habit of growth.

1 A basket with insert and lining.

3 Carefully thread the plants through the wall.

2 Cover only the bottom with the lining.

4 Wrap moss around the neck of the root.

Using young plants

Advantages: They are well priced. The small rootstocks are easy to insert through the mesh of the wire.
Disadvantages: It will take longer from planting to flowering. There is a smaller selection of these in the gardening trade than of ready-grown, mature plants.

Using mature plants

Advantages: The gardening trade offers a large selection of plants. The plants flower faster.
Disadvantages: They are more expensive and have larger rootstocks. A few special tips will help with planting:
● Pull the wire mesh apart a little so that there is more room to insert the plants.
● Cut the wire open using wire cutters.
● Larger plants can be carefully divided if several of them are growing in one pot.

Preparing the basket

(illustrations 1 and 2) You can prepare the basket in two different ways.

1 First, completely cover the inside of the basket with a prepared insert (see illustration 1), moss or coconut fibre, then lay in the liner. The insert will hide the liner and prevent the compost from falling through the planting holes. Planting will require some deftness as each plant has to be pushed through narrow holes made in the two layers.

2 The neck of the root of each plant is surrounded with moss or coconut fibre after the plant has been inserted. No liner is used to line the inside of the basket before you start, but it is added gradually as you insert the plants. The disadvantage with this method is that the compost may dry out faster.

My tip: Cover the floor of the basket with coconut fibre or moss and liner, covering the

5 *An attractive wall bracket will complement a hanging basket.*

inside to a height of about 5 cm (2 in) (see illustration 2). This "dish" will hold water and also prevent it from running through and dripping away when watering. Do not make any holes in the insert and start planting above it. You can also insert a saucer or something similar in a very flat basket.

Special ways of planting

(illustrations 3 and 4) There are two possibilities.

1 Carefully wrap the plant quite tightly in foil or cellophane, taking care not to damage any part of the plant, and insert it through the basket mesh shoots-first, from the inside to the outside (see illustration 3).

2 Insert it rootstock-first from the outside inwards.

How to plant

Hang the basket up at chest height, then prepare it as above. Remove the plants from their pots. Water dry plants first.

Planting should always be done from the bottom upwards; i.e. plant the floor of the basket first.

● Cut a slit in the insert for each plant.

● Push the plant through the mesh and insert it to the beginning of the stalk. Close the opening around the neck of the root (see illustration 4). Distribute half of the plants in this way at the bottom of the basket.

● Sprinkle compost between the roots and press down. Repeat the procedure at the top and water.

Design tip (see illustration 5): When the basket has been freshly planted it will look untidy. This will sort itself out after a few days once the shoot tips and leaves begin to turn towards the light.

Hanging flowers

Containers can be found in many shapes and styles.

Plant containers

You can obtain plant containers in many different materials.

Ceramic containers: Plants look particularly good in earth-coloured or terracotta hanging containers. Unglazed containers promote the growth of roots as the walls of the vessel are porous; this also means, however, that water will evaporate more quickly and the compost will dry out faster. Colourful glazed containers are an additional decoration for your plant collections. Their great weight renders large ceramic containers very stable. Hanging containers should be safely secured because of their weight (see p. 16/17).

Stoneware containers: Stoneware boxes are available everywhere in the gardening trade. They are tip-proof, frost-proof and allow the roots to breath.

Plastic containers: They are ideal for hanging plants because of their light weight and because they do not break easily. They retain moisture in the compost as their walls are not porous. They tend to be rather unattractive but the sides are soon covered up by hanging plants.

Wooden boxes, willow baskets: Containers made of natural materials, like wooden boxes (see pp. 27 and 31), fruit crates (see p. 35) or willow baskets, make attractive plant containers which harmonize with the plants. Their durability is, however, rather limited because of constant moisture from watering. The life of wooden containers can be extended by applying a protective coat of paint or plant-friendly wood preserver. Another possibility is to line the inside with polythene sheeting (do not forget to make holes to allow water to run away!). The same goes for baskets made out of any natural materials. The baskets should be checked frequently as both the floor and handles may rot away.

Semi-spherical-shaped containers for planting against a wall: These containers, made of terracotta (see photo, p. 22) or plastic, are very suitable as an ornament on a wall and will not take up much space. Baskets of the same shape can also be obtained.

NB: Every container will require a drainage hole so that rainwater or regular water is not stored inside the containers to waterlog the plants.

Holders for single pots: Potholders made of wire are also obtainable for single pots (see p. 42).

Complying with the law

If you own your house, you should be able to use your balcony or patio in whatever way you see fit. If you own or are living in an apartment which has a balcony you must make sure that anything you do does not infringe upon the rights of, nor endanger or inconvenience, your landlord, other tenants or the general public. As a rule, with the exception of the outside façade, a tenant may secure plant containers to balcony railings or on a patio and install plants in them, provided this is done safely.
NB: Check the weight-carrying capacity of the balcony.
A few important points should be considered if you are a tenant:

Environmentally friendly containers made of recycled material.

● Before securing boxes to the outside of balcony railings, check whether your tenancy agreement expressly permits this, otherwise the landlord may prohibit such use. If you own your apartment, there may also be rules of usage governing the installation of plant containers on the property.

● Make sure you secure the plant containers in such a fashion that even a storm will not tear them from their anchoring. Use balcony box fixtures with a safety lip (see p. 17).

● Only use chains, ropes, hooks and dowels with sufficient carrying capacity for holding up hanging containers and baskets. The weight will increase dramatically when the plants are being watered. As a guide, use the weight data in the design section (see pp. 18-43).

● Suspend hanging containers or baskets only from galvanized chains or wires or plastic-coated ropes. Untreated chains or wires may rust under the influence of moisture (watering, rain) and come away. Ropes made of natural fibre may rot and break.

● Check all fixtures at regular intervals.

● Make sure that water dripping down does not damage the façade or run on to a neighbouring property or on to the street below. Always stand a bowl under plants you are watering (see illustration, p. 54).

● Only ever spray plants with protective agents when there is no wind. Always make sure that spray mist cannot drift on to a neighbouring balcony.

Making and securing your own containers

You can easily make your own original hanging flowerbed or vegetable garden without a great deal of technical expertise.

Hanging plant bed
(illustrations 1 and 2)

A base for a hanging bed that can then be covered, according to your taste, with containers and plants is easily and quickly assembled without a great deal of technical knowledge and using parts obtainable from most builders' yards. You will only require tools for securing it to the ceiling.

When purchasing parts, you should make sure that they all have the correct carrying capacity (after watering, the bed will weigh about 18 kg or 40 lb). Also make sure that the parts fit together before you begin.

Equipment
● 1 metal grid, as used for scraping shoes or for covering cellar window pits. Grids like this can be obtained in various different sizes. If you intend using a fruit crate as a plant container, one measuring 40 cm x 60 cm (16 x 24 in) will be large enough.

● 4 circular steel-link chains (length 100 cm or 40 in each) with a carrying capacity of at least 18 kg (40 lb). Have the pieces of chain cut to size when you purchase them.
● 4 S-hooks for attaching the chains securely to the metal grid.
● 1 adjustable chain link with thread (see illustration 5) to gather the four chains together at the top.
● 1 block and tackle (see p. 55) for lowering and raising the plants for watering.

> **My tip:**
> Galvanized or painted parts will last longer.

Assembling the hanging bed

● Attach a chain to each corner of the metal grid using an S-hook.
● Gather the four chains together at the top by means of an adjustable link.
● Attach the block and tackle to the ceiling and fix the rope.
● Suspend the hanging bed from the block and tackle.

Safe anchorage
(illustrations 3-6)

The anchoring point on a ceiling or wall has to carry a considerable weight. Depending on the materials from which the wall or ceiling is made, the possibilities for securing attachments may vary.

1 A colourfully painted fruit box makes an attractive plant container.

2 An S-hook attaches a chain to the metal grid.

3 Balcony box fixture with safety lip.

4 Rope clamps secure the ends of the rope.

5 Adjustable chain link with screw fixture.

case of open balconies (or on a pergola etc.), wrap a chain or plastic-coated rope around the beam and attach the plant container to this. Take extra care with wooden ceilings or walls as the carrying capacity of panels is very low and a screw-in hook will only be adequate for a very lightweight plant container. It would be better to bore right through the wood and insert a dowel in the concrete or stone behind it.

● Wall fixtures, like ornamental hooks and brackets (see p. 13), should always be supported at the bottom and secured with further screws.

● Fixtures with safety lips can be obtained for balcony boxes (see illustration 3). These will prevent the box from tipping off.

Various other aids will also help to secure hanging containers. **S-shaped hooks** can be used to connect a chain attached to the container and the actual chain used for suspension. They are also useful for other joins. They come in many different sizes. **Rope clamps** (see illustration 4) can be used to fix the ends of wires and plastic-coated ropes. They can be obtained for different gauges of rope.

Adjustable chain links (see illustration 5) are single chain links that can be opened on one side and closed again. They are excellent for gathering several chains together.

● Always use plastic-coated dowels to install fixtures in brick or rendered walls or ceilings (see illustration 6). They can be obtained in various sizes. Use a drill to bore a hole of the correct thickness and length for the dowel (always use a masonry bit), insert the dowel in the hole (if necessary gently tap it in with a hammer) and screw the hook into the dowel. Before drilling, make sure there are no electric cables underneath. If you are not used to handling a drill, it is better to let a professional do the job as you could be in danger of injuring yourself!

● If you are making a hole in a massive wooden beam, use a screw-in hook. In the

6 A dowel holds the hook securely in the ceiling.

Stylish ideas

With a little basic knowledge about gardening and a lot of imagination, a beautiful display of plants can be created in almost any position. Check through the suggestions in the following pages.

Photo above: Gazania displays its full beauty in sunlight.
Photo left: With the right aids, such as polythene, coconut fibre and the correct tools, it is not difficult to design an attractive hanging basket.

Stylish ideas

The right position is most important

Before buying your plants, you should take a very good look at the position in which you are intending to grow them. Whether they thrive will not depend entirely on water and nutrients but also on the light and the prevailing climatic conditions they will be asked to live in. Different plants have different requirements with respect to light, temperature, wind and rain. To make the choice of plants for your intended position easier, the following design ideas for groups of plants have been arranged for plants that prefer sunny, semi-shady and shady positions. The special requirements of free-hanging planting arrangements have also been taken into consideration. The exposed nature of the planting containers means that it is sometimes easier to care for some sun-loving plants in semi-shady conditions and that they will grow even more luxuriantly there. Before deciding, you should be clear in your own mind which conditions prevail on your balcony, patio, etc.

● Which direction does the position face?
● Is there a roof or awning over the intended position or do trees or a house wall protect the position from direct sunlight?
● What are wind and rain conditions like?

Plants for sunny positions

Spring planting
pansies (*Viola wittrockiana* hybrids)
daisies (*Bellis perennis*)
bulbous plants such as tulips (*Tulipa*)
narcissi (*Narcissus*)
crocuses (*Crocus*)

Summer planting
Gazania hybrids
Livingstone daisies (*Dorotheanthus bellidiformis*)
portulaca (*Portulaca*)
Swan River daisies (*Brachycome iberidifolia*)
pelargoniums (*Pelargonium*)
petunias (*Petunia* hybrids) ☻☠
fleabane (*Erigeron karvinskianus*)
Scaevola saligna

Autumn planting
violets (*Viola cornuta* hybrids)
heather (*Erica herbacea*)
chrysanthemums (*Dendranthema grandiflorum* hybrids)
ivy (*Hedera helix*) ☠

A sunny position

South-facing balconies, patios or roof gardens are typically the sunniest positions, which also means that there is a lot of heat during the day in the summer and, depending on the position, the air may not move much. Sensitive plants may burn here. In all cases, you will have to water a great deal. If you are not sure whether you will always be able to water frequently, you should go for a particularly robust selection of plants (see p. 23) or consider the installation of semi-automatic or automatic irrigation.

Positions that face south east or south west should be less vulnerable to such extreme conditions. The same goes for a situation where a tree, a house wall opposite or a roof protects the plants from too much sunlight. The position is classified as shady if the balcony is facing south but has a roof or something similar which keeps the sun off completely. This fact should be reflected in your choice of plants (for plants that like shady positions, see pp. 36-43).

Look at the chosen site at various times during the day as conditions may alter as the sun moves round.

A herb basket above the table releases its spicy scent.

An exotic blend of colours

This is where plants from hot, dry climatic zones meet up. All the plants in this basket enjoy plenty of heat and lots of sunshine and can also manage on little water – ideal for a sunny position. They will not mind if they do not receive water regularly on schedule as they either have a built-in water reservoir or a special talent for using up the precious liquid frugally. In their countries of origin they have evolved to cope with long periods of drought.

Plants for a wire basket with a diameter of 35 cm (14 in):
5 gazania (*Gazania* hybrids)
3 Livingstone daisies (*Dorotheanthus bellidiformis*)
4 portulaca (*Portulaca*)
2 convolvulous (*Convolvulus sabatius*)
Total weight of the group: 10 kg (22 lb).

Planting and care
All plants can be bought from the last month of spring onwards. You can increase the number of different colours in your arrangement if you use varieties that come in a range of colours. *Gazania*, *Dorotheanthus* and *Portulaca* are usually planted several to a pot in nurseries and often produce several different colours in one pot. Prepare the wire basket and insert the plants (see pp. 12/13). Plant a *Convolvulus sabatius* at both the front and the back of the bottom of the basket. Its long, trailing shoots will look best growing freely downwards. Towards the top of the basket alternate *Gazania, Dorotheanthus* and *Portulaca*. Water the basket well (place a bowl underneath!) and keep it as evenly moist as possible. Fertilize weekly. Cut out any dead and faded flowers and foliage as this will encourage the formation of new flowers. These plants react sensitively to continuous rain and waterlogging. During longer periods of wet weather, it is a good

Terracotta wall container.

Terracotta hanging container.

idea to protect the arrangement from too much moisture by hanging the basket underneath an overhanging roof.

For people who are away from home all day
The glowing, colourful flowers of these plants are open only during the day and when the sun is shining. If you are not at home all day, you should probably choose plants whose flowers are open all the time (see the flower swing, pp. 30/31).

Choice of colours
Plants originating from regions with plenty of sunshine are often very brightly coloured. If you like strong colours, you can combine them with complementary colours. If you feel this would create too much of a garish splash, you can also use a combination of quieter shades or tones.

Design tip
The plants used here will also suit smaller containers with very little compost in them. They are ideal for summertime plantings in ceramic hanging containers or half-bowl-shaped containers made of terracotta.

Compact and full of colour.

An aromatic herb basket

Plants with highly scented flowers or leaves are always a pleasure for the senses. Honey melon sage, lemon thyme and curry plant provide a real feast of wonderful aromas. As these plants are usually to be found growing on the ground, it is generally necessary to bend down to enjoy the full impact of their scent as you crush their leaves and flowerheads in your fingers.

However, if you plant various scented plants in a hanging basket and suspend this at nose level, the plants will release their pleasant perfume at just the right height. If you suspend the basket using a block and tackle, you can even go a step further and vary the level at which the plants hang (see p. 55).

In addition, an airy position like this is the ideal place to grow kitchen herbs with superb flavours. It will make things even easier still if you hang the basket right beside an outdoor table on your

Most herbs have very delicate flowers.

Pocket amphora

balcony or patio, then you can pick the herbs fresh to eat with your meal. Depending on the plants chosen, such a combination of plants can prove quite robust if subjected to short-term periods of drought (see plant list, p. 25).

24

Plants for a wire basket with a diameter of 35 cm (14 in):
2 honey melon sage (*Salvia elegans*)
1 sage (*Salvia officinalis* "Tricolor")
1 golden sage (*Salvia officinalis* "Aurea")
1 scented-leafed pelargonium with an aroma of nutmeg and white/green variegated leaves (*Pelargonium fragrans* "Variegata")
1 scented pelargonium with a fruit scent and red leaves
1 curry plant (*Helichrysum italicum*)
1 hyssop with pink flowers (*Hyssopus officinalis*)
2 large quaking grass (*Briza maxima*)
2 lemon thyme (*Thymus x citriodorus*)
These plants are not commonly available everywhere but you should be able to purchase them through mail-order nurseries (see sources, p. 60).

An alternative collection

If you want to grow your own herb garden in a hurry, you can fall back on the usual kitchen herbs, for example basil (*Ocimum basilicum*), marjoram (*Majorana hortensis*), dill (*Anthemum graveolens*) or parsley (*Petroselinum crispum*). These herbs not only smell nice but can also be used to give flavour in cooking.

My tip: Hanging baskets can even be transformed into vegetable gardens (see photo, p. 8) if they are planted all the way round with young vegetable plants. Total weight of the arrangement: 8 kg (18 lb).

Planting and care

Plant after the last frosts in the last month of spring. Prepare the basket (see pp. 12/13). Honey melon sage needs the most room so plant one of these to the right and left of the bottom of the basket wall. Between these, at the front and back, plant lemon thyme which grows in cushions. Distribute the other herbs all over the basket.

Fill up all the empty spaces between the plants with compost. Press the compost down and water the basket well. Fertilize regularly (see fertilizing vegetables, p. 46). If you have the space available, you can overwinter this arrangement in a frost-free room during the winter months (see overwintering, pp. 56/57) as all these plants are perennials. Cut the plants back before overwintering them.

My tip: Honey melon sage (*Salvia elegans*) has a profusion of foliage and requires lots of water. If you are unable to water regularly, it would be better to choose a plant that does not mind a bit of dryness or else hang the basket in a semi-shady position.

The following plants require *less water* than most:
sage (*Salvia officinalis*), rosemary (*Rosmarinus officinalis*)
lavender (*Lavandula angustifolia*)
oregano (*Origanum vulgare*)
marjoram (*Majorana hortensis*)
sedum (*Sedum reflexum*)
various species of thyme (*Thymus*)
cotton lavender (*Santolina chamaecyparissus*)
winter savory (*Satureja montana*)

Tip on containers

Ceramic pocket amphorae present an attractive possibility for overhanging plantings. You can plant herbs or even strawberry plants in the pockets. These containers are also sold under the name of strawberry pots in the gardening trade.

Be aware that the larger strawberry barrels do become very heavy when planted up. They can become impossible to move or lift, so you must decide where you wish to place the pot or barrel before you plant it up.

Stylish ideas

Strawberry fair

By growing the right varieties of strawberries and giving a little extra care, you can be certain of a rich harvest of fruit over several months. The lovely white flowers also make an attractive feature. The strawberry plants ensure their own propagation by producing long runners which form tiny new strawberry plants. These young plants look very pretty when they produce flowers at the ends of the runners, followed by fruit. A rustic tub made of light oak looks superb when full of strawberry plants.

Plants for a container with a diameter of 30 cm (12 in):
1-5 strawberry plants (*Fragaria*)
The best plants for this arrangement are hanging or climbing strawberries which will be found on sale in the gardening trade from the last month of spring into the first month of summer. These types flower and produce fruit all summer long. They are sold as large container plants or as small young plants. The number of plants you will require for a planting in a wooden container will depend on the size of the individual plants. If you cannot find any plants to buy during these months you will certainly be able to obtain them during the last month of summer which is the best planting time for garden strawberries.

An alternative suggestion

The small Alpine strawberries make a dainty ornament as well as producing tasty fruit. If you wish to grow the fruit only as a visual delight, you can also use the "fake" strawberry (*Duchesnea indica*). This grows vigorously; its fruits are the same size as wild strawberries but have no flavour. The flowers are yellow.

Total weight of the planting: 17 kg (37 lb). Make sure the attachment is particularly strong and secure as this container is a considerable weight.

Planting and care

Before planting, check whether the container is equipped with drainage holes.
Place a drainage layer in the bottom of the container, for example clay pellets (Hortag), to a level of about 5 cm (2 in) and then cover this layer with permeable fabric. This drainage layer will not only protect your plants from the effects of waterlogging but will also reduce the overall weight of the planting. If you want to reduce the weight even more, you can double the thickness of the drainage layer.
Fill the remainder of the container with compost and plant the strawberry plants. Press the compost down so that the rootstocks are well covered with compost on all sides and then water well. If the runners of the strawberry plants become too long, they can be trimmed. Fertilize strawberries in the same way as herbs and vegetables (see p. 46).
Depending on the variety, strawberries are particularly susceptible to mildew if the humidity is high and temperatures are constantly changing (see p. 50). To build up the plants' immunity, and as a preventive, we recommend watering your plants regularly during the growth period with mare's tail brew, nettle brew, comfrey brew or yarrow brew, all of which contain silicic acid (see p. 52).
You will receive years of pleasure from this arrangement if you position it in a sheltered spot outside or overwinter it indoors at no more than 5°C (41°F) (see p. 56).

Securing containers

If the wooden container has no means of attachment, drill three holes at equal intervals in the top of one of its walls and insert S-hooks.

Make sure the distance between the holes and the top edge of the container is great enough to prevent the wood from giving way. Hang a circular-link steel chain from each hole. Gather the three chains together at the top with an S-hook or an adjustable chain link.

Wooden barrel.

Tip on containers
Do-it-yourself enthusiasts may wish to transform an old wooden barrel into a strawberry barrel. A particularly attractive effect is created if the strawberry plants do not just cascade out of the top of the barrel but also out of additional holes that can be sawn into the walls of the barrel.

Strawberries make an attractive arrangement.

27

Stylish ideas

A semi-shady position

These sites are characterized by receiving plenty of light but without constant, aggressive, intense rays from the sun. Burning noontime sunlight should generally be avoided. On the other hand, this sort of position does not mean that the plants are sitting in deep shadow. Semi-shady positions are generally east- or west-facing. An east-facing balcony receives softer morning sunlight. A west-facing balcony receives rays from the afternoon and evening sun but, being the side more exposed to weather, it may often be battered by storms and rain. Your hanging containers should, therefore, be very well secured in west-facing positions. In all cases, the prevailing conditions on site should be considered. Even south-facing balconies in full sunlight, or shady north-facing ones, may become semi-shady if, for example, a tree blocks out the sunlight or a neighbouring house wall reflects the sun's rays.

Choosing plants

A semi-shady position is ideal for hanging plants as the relatively small amount of compost in the containers will not dry out so fast. On the other hand, sun-loving plants will thrive here just as much as in a sunny position.

Plants for semi-shady positions

Spring planting
forget-me-nots (*Myosotis sylvatica*)
pansies (*Viola wittrockiana* hybrids)
double daisies (*Bellis perennis*)
primulas (*Primula vulgaris* hybrids)

Summer planting
black-eyed Susan (*Thunbergia alata*)
morning glory (*Ipomoea*)
climbing nasturtium (*Tropaeolum peregrinum*)
nasturtium (*Tropaeolum majus*)
Lotus berthelotii
pelargonium (*Pelargonium*)
lobelia (*Lobelia erinus*)
begonia (*Begonia semperflorens* hybrid)
tuber begonia (*Begonia – tuber begonia hybrids*)
Calceolaria integrifolia

Autumn planting
heather (*Calluna vulgaris*)
autumn asters (*Aster*), various species

As you can see from these lists, with simple care you can take full advantage of a suitable position to grow a wide range of plants. Plants that form lots of leaves in a very short time do particularly well in a semi-shady position. Among these are a wide selection of climbing plants.

Symbols used in the gardening trade

Bought plants often have labels attached to them. These labels bear symbols giving the requirements of the plant with respect to position and light.

○ **sun:** This plant requires, or can cope with, full sunlight and heat, even at noon. A completely sunny, south-facing position will be necessary for the production of plenty of flowers.

◖ **semi-shade:** This plant requires a bright position without intense midday sunlight. Morning and evening sunlight, i.e. east- and west-facing positions, are ideal for this plant. Even light shade is suitable for growing this sort of plant.

● **shade:** This plant can cope with, or prefers, shade.

This hanging basket provides an attractive visual screen.

Stylish ideas

A colourful flower swing

Traditional balcony flowers in glowing colours create a wonderful effect from a distance. The hanging varieties are also excellent for trailing over a balcony railing. Using an interesting or original container, you can place these easily cared-for, continuous-flowering plants in a free-hanging position.

Plants for a box 70 cm (28 in) long:
1 hanging pelargonium (*Pelargonium peltatum* hybrids)
1 *Bidens ferufolia*
5 nasturtiums (*Tropaeolum majus*)
1 *Scaevola saligna*
Total weight of the planting: 20 kg (44 lb)

Planting and care
Scaevola saligna, *Bidens ferufolia* and hanging perlargoniums can be bought as ready-to-plant plants from the last month of spring onwards in nurseries and garden centres. Nasturtiums can be obtained in the form of young plants or you can grow them

yourself from seed. Fill a third of the box with compost. Place the pelargonium on the left, the *Bidens* and the *Scaevola* in the centre and the nasturtiums on the right. Fill the box with compost, press down and water well. Nasturtiums will flower more profusely and produce fewer leaves if you do not fertilize them too often. In order that the other plants will receive an adequate amount of fertilizer, use controlled-release fertilizer or fertilizer sticks in a targeted way around their root systems (see p. 46). In this way you can avoid the use of liquid fertilizer. Regularly remove dead flowers and leaves. If the nasturtiums threaten to smother the other

Heather in a pot.

plants, cut them back a little.

Securing the container
Balcony railings: You can attach the box of plants to the railings with special fixtures (see illustration 3, p. 17).
Free-hanging: If you wish to suspend the balcony box from the ceiling you will require an overbox (paint it to protect it from rotting) which you can build yourself with a bit of experience or have a carpenter build for you. Make sure it has an attachment which you can easily make yourself.
● Stand the balcony box in a rather wider box made of heavy wood. Allow a gap of 3 cm (1¼ in) between the inner and outer boxes so·that the inner one can be removed easily.
● Make sure that both the inner and outer boxes are equipped with drainage holes.
● Stand the box on narrow wooden battens so that excess water can run away unhindered.
● Take two narrow-

gauge iron pipes, which correspond in length to the width of the overbox, and pass them underneath each end of the overbox; insert chains through these pipes and suspend the box from the chains (see photo below).
My tip: If you wish to grow perennial plants, insert a layer of polystyrene between the two boxes as protection against the cold.

Colour tip
If you enjoy the pink shades of pelargoniums during the summer, you can have the same colours again in the autumn by using winter heather.

Flowerbox attachment.

A free-hanging balcony box on chains.

Visual screens

This basket is enveloped in luxuriantly growing plants that will produce long shoots and dense foliage in the shortest period of time. It is simply overflowing with eye-catching nasturtiums and various varieties of *Asarina barclaiana*. The latter are distant relatives of the snapdragon and are generally grown as climbing plants.

Nasturtiums.

If no climbing aids are present, the long, trailing shoots will hang down over the edge of the container. This basket provides a dense visual screen and an eyecatching decoration all in one (see photograph, p. 29).

This cascade of flowers forms an attractive visual screen.

Plants for a wire basket with a diameter of 40 cm (16 in):
3 climbing nasturtiums (*Tropaeolum peregrinum*)
2 nasturtiums (*Tropaeolum majus*)
2 hanging pelargoniums (*Pelargonium peltatum* hybrids)
1 ground ivy with white and green variegated leaves (*Glechoma hederacea* "Variegata")
2 *Asarina barclaiana*
2 *Asarina scandens*
1 *Rhodochiton atrosanguineus*
1 convolvulus (*Convolvulus sabatius*)
3 coleus (*Coleus blumei* hybrids)
Total weight of the planting: 18 kg (40 lb).

Planting and care

The right time to plant is after the last frosts, about the middle of the last month of spring. You can purchase the plants in nurseries and garden centres or grow them yourself from seed during the middle of the second month of spring. Prepare the basket and plant it (see pp. 12/13). All the plants, with the exception of pelargoniums and coleus, can be distributed evenly on the base and walls of the basket. Only the colourful coleus and pelargoniums should be placed in the upper portion and on the surface of the basket. When planting, make sure that the spaces between the rootstocks are completely filled with compost.
Water the basket well; after three weeks use a liquid flower fertilizer once weekly.
If one of the plants begins to dominate the arrangement, cut back its shoots. You can break up this arrangement before the first frosts in the autumn. Plant the pelargoniums, convolvulus and coleus in individual pots and overwinter them in a frost-free position.

My tip: To help the climbing plants to produce a more bushy appearance after planting them in the basket, pinch out the tips of the first shoots. This will encourage the formation of plenty of lateral shoots.

Morning glory sown from seed.

Design tip

If you want to cover a wall or the railing of a balcony or patio with greenery but do not have enough room on the ground or floor for a large plant container, you can hang a basket of climbing plants near a trellis or balcony railing. Carefully tie the long shoots from the basket to the railing. The plants in the basket will then climb all over the trellis or railing throughout the summer. When positioning the basket, remember that once its climbing shoots are entwined around a support, you will no longer be able move the basket about. This means hanging it up in such a way that it is easy to reach for watering.

An alternative planting

To obtain a cheap planting for your hanging basket, after the last frosts in late spring, sow morning glory (*Ipomoea*) seed or runner beans (*Phaseolus coccineus*) directly into a basket filled with compost or into a ceramic hanging container. Keep the compost evenly moist during germination. After about ten days, the plants will begin to germinate and, throughout the entire summer, will grow all over the container. The *Ipomoea* has brilliant blue flowers and the runner bean flowers are an intense scarlet.

Stylish ideas

A hanging vegetable garden

You can plant a vegetable garden in a very small space in this way. The basic construction is simple and you can put it together from parts that can be found in any builder's yard. The actual plant container is made from a painted fruit box that can easily be purchased at a weekly market or in a greengrocers. Naturally, if you do not wish to grow vegetables, this hanging garden can be filled with flowering plants instead.

Plants for an orange box of the dimensions 60 x 40 cm (24 x 16 in):
1 cherry tomato plant
1 red cabbage
3 lettuce plants (choose varieties with different leaf colours and shapes)
1 gourd
red basil plants
Total weight of the planting (inc. the metal grid): 16 kg (35 lb).

Securing the container
This hanging bed requires a basic construction comprising four chains and an attached metal grid (see p. 16). It will be easier to care for the plants if it can be lowered for watering. A block and tackle arrangement should be installed for this purpose (see p. 55).

Planting and care
You can start to plant after the last frost at the end of spring. You will find a large selection of young vegetable plants in the gardening trade at this time. Use a fruit box, preferably with high walls, as this will ensure a large volume of compost for the plants. Give the box a coat of paint before planting as this will make your arrangement more attractive. Allow the paint to dry properly and then line the inside of the box with polythene sheeting. Cut several holes in the bottom of the sheet so that excess water can run out. Before planting, fill the box with compost and insert the plants. Place the red cabbage at the front so that it inclines forward, plant the tomato on the left and then place the other young plants between them.
You can sow the lettuce seeds in the gaps and harvest them before the other vegetables have grown very big. The lettuces will germinate quickly and produce salad leaves. In addition, they will later produce pretty, creamy-white, star-shaped flowers that look enchanting among the other plants. After three weeks, fertilize the vegetable garden weekly (see p. 46). Check for pests regularly.

My tip: Cherry tomatoes do not have to be tied to sticks. They produce very attractive yellow flowers and their miniature, brilliant red fruits are quite eyecatching.

Positioning
If you place this arrangement beside an outside table, you can pick fresh tomatoes straight from the plant to eat with your meal. Cress is also ideal for this method of growing or you could even sow a whole boxful of lettuces. Naturally, this kind of hanging bed can also be filled with herbs (see p. 24).

Water melon.

Aubergine.

Design tip
Vegetables can produce
a very attractive effect.
The creamy-coloured
flowers of lettuce can be
very ornamental.
These flowers are formed
when the lettuce "bolts"
and the flowerhead
shoots up.
Water melons and
aubergines also make
interesting and very tasty
additions to your hanging
vegetable garden.

*Line the inside of the
box with polythene.*

A painted fruit box makes a good container.

Stylish ideas

A shady position

A shady site requires just as careful a choice of plants as a sunny one. North-facing positions are perpetually in the shade as direct sunlight will never reach them. However, even a square courtyard or a planting position directly under a tree with dense foliage will create very shady spots. Because there is less sunlight in shady positions, the plants placed there and the surface of the compost in the container tend to lose less water through evaporation. This means that moisture is retained for longer in the compost. One advantage of this is that the plants do not need to be watered so often. On the other hand, there is a disadvantage if the plants become waterlogged as this may cause damage to the roots (see p. 53). Although there is a smaller selection of plants that feel at home in a shady position, with a little careful thought you can still have a profusion of summery flowers on your north-facing balcony. You can also resort to short-term decoration by using plants that can be replaced with others when they have finished flowering. This sort of short-term use is best achieved by standing the plant in its pot inside the hanging container. This will enable you to exchange it for another easily and quickly.

Plants for shady positions

Spring planting
forget-me-nots (*Myosotis sylvatica*)
primulas (*Primula vulgaris* hybrids)
spring anemones (*Anemone blanda*) ☠

Summer planting
tuber begonias (*Begonia –* tuber begonia hybrids) ☠
ivy (*Hedera helix*) ☠
Tradescantia
Chlorophytum comosum
Mimulus luteus
fuchsias (*Fuchsia* hybrids)
busy Lizzie (*Impatiens walleriana*)

Autumn planting
heather (*Erica heracea*)
heather (*Calluna vulgaris*)
autumn asters (*Aster*), various species
forget-me-nots (*Myosotis sylvatica*)
Gaultheria procumbens
chrysanthemums (*Dendranthema grandiflorum* hybrids)

My tip: Have fun experimenting with a selection of plants as many plants are very adaptable. Some sun-loving plants will still produce flowers in the shade although they do not develop quite so profusely.

Reaching for the light

Sunlight is vital for plants so they tend always to grow towards the source of light and will produce most flowers in sunny conditions. The part of the plant that is furthest from light tends to become bare and often becomes unsightly. Positions that are not built up and obtain light from all sides are, therefore, ideal for the creation of attractive, all-round plantings. In order to encourage this ideal all-round growth in unfavourable conditions, for example on a cramped balcony that is roofed over, one method is to paint the walls etc. white. You should not continually turn an arrangement to expose all sides of it to the light. This creates great stress for the plant and hinders its growth.

A profusion of plants can be grown even in a shady position.

Stylish ideas

Baskets of begonias and fuchsias

This elegant basket arrangement, containing hanging begonias in shades of pink and apricot amid variegated green and white foliage, will bring clusters of flowering colour to even the shadiest nook (see photograph, p. 37). The small-flowering fuchsias are ideal for shady positions. Although they are true children of the sun, mint, scented-leaved pelargoniums and ground ivy with its aromatic foliage will quickly become accustomed to a shady position.

Plants for a wire basket with a diameter of 35 cm (14 in):
2 hanging begonias (*Begonia* – tuber begonia hybrids)
3 hanging fuchsias (*Fuchsia magellanica*)
1 *Rhodochiton atrosanguineus*
3 ground ivy (*Glechoma hederacea* "Variegata")
2 pineapple mint (*Mentha suaveolens* "Variegata")
2 *Chlorophytum comosum*

2 scented-leafed pelargoniums with a scent of peppermint (*Pelargonium tomentosum*)
Total weight of the planting: 12 kg (26 lb).

Planting and care
Plant after the last frosts at the end of spring. The plants for this pretty combination can be bought at garden centres and nurseries or from mail-order firms (see sources, p. 60). This arrangement will take its overall balance from a subtle combination of different shapes of growth (see p. 9). The graceful curtain of foliage (see photograph, p. 57) and downward-trailing shoots have their stable base in the compact, bushy plants at the top of the basket. Prepare the wire basket and install the plants (see pp. 12/13). In the lower and middle levels of the basket, plant ground ivy and *Rhodochiton atrosanguineus* alternated with scented-leafed pelargoniums and hanging fuchsias. Distribute the remaining plants at the top near the walls of the basket and over the surface. Water the plants well and begin fertilizing three weeks later. Pick out dead flowerheads and leaves. The more vigorously growing plants, like mint and pelargonium, should be lightly cut back from time to time if they start crowding the other plants.

My tip: Mint can be obtained in many different varieties. Not only do the many types of mint have differently scented leaves but they also grow vigorously and have interesting, attractive foliage. You can also use them as herbs in cooking. If you cannot find any pineapple mint in the gardening trade but still wish to have variegated green and white decorative foliage, try planting *Plectranthus*, which is easier to obtain, or simply use an ivy (*Hedera*) with variegated leaves.

Colour
Hanging begonias come in many different colours, from deep red and glowing yellow to delicate pink and white, and with double and single blooms. All pastel shades go well with the variegated green and white leaves of ground ivy and pineapple mint. A particularly enchanting effect can be obtained with a combination of apricot and pink or by mixing different shades of pink. You could design your basket entirely in shades of one colour if you add white tuber begonias and fuchsias to the white and green foliage. If in doubt, you should go for fewer colours in a combination and plant flowers of each colour in one or two larger groups.

A profusion of fuchsias

Fuchsias are wonderfully adaptable plants to use in designing baskets and hanging containers. The hanging fuchsias are best for this mode of

Pineapple mint.

planting. The colours, sizes and shapes of the flowers of the hanging varieties are just as varied as those of the upright-growing varieties, for example "La Campanella" (white/violet), "Elfriede Ott" (salmon/pink) or "Annabel" (white).

The scented-leafed pelargoniums spread an aroma of peppermint.

39

Stylish ideas

Bellflowers and grasses

Experiment by planting unusual plants in an unusual container. For example, here a small selection of woodland plants have been grown in a section of guttering as an interesting and novel hanging box that is perfect for a shady patio or balcony. All the plants shown here are perennials and the arrangement can be kept outside during the winter.

Plants for a section of guttering with a length of 70 cm (28 in):
2 large selfheal (*Prunella grandiflora*)
3 yellow corydalis (*Corydalis lutea*)
1 giant bellflower (*Campanula latifolia*)
1 barrenwort or bishop's hat (*Epimedium x rubrum*)
2 tufted hairgrass (*Deschampsia cespitosa*)
1 periwinkle with green/white leaves (*Vinca major* "Variegata")
Total weight of the planting: 8 kg (18 lb).

This guttering container can be filled with woodland plants.

Making the plant container

The container consists of one section of roof guttering, with two end pieces to close both ends of the gutter and chains for suspending it. The best solution is to let a plumber or DIY expert put it together for you. Guttering comes in several different widths and the measurements do not refer to the diameter of the gutter itself but to the width of the metal/plastic/PVC etc. before it is bent into a gutter shape.

Wall attachment.

The best gutters for this purpose are those made of metal or stout PVC that are about 33 cm (13¼ in) wide before shaping. They will hold more compost and the plants will do better. Avoid waterlogging by drilling several holes in the bottom of the gutter. The finished bed will be suspended on chains, so holes for these have to be made at both ends, front and back, about 2 cm (¾ in) below the upper edge, using a drill. Insert an S-hook in each hole to which you can attach the chains.

An alternative method

Wire ropes can be used instead of chains. Push a piece of wire through a hole drilled in the guttering from the outside, draw it along the inside wall of the guttering and push it out through another hole drilled at the other end. Repeat this along the other side of the guttering.

My tip: The most attractive gutters are those made of galvanized metal that will not rust. Copper gutters are only suitable for planting if they have been coated with bitumen on the inside. Plastic and PVC gutters are also obtainable in the trade. They are not as attractive as the metal ones but can be painted any colour you like. They have the advantage of being less heavy when planted up but do remember to use a robust plastic gutter.

Planting and care

Hardy perennials can be bought all year round in garden centres and nurseries. The best time to plant is during the first two months of spring, which gives the plants time to acclimatize well before the autumn so that they can face the winter months with a well-developed root system. A particularly interesting effect is obtained with this kind of arrangement if you distribute tall and low-growing plants unevenly along the gutter, for example by creating a focal point at the right end with taller plants. Place a few low-growing plants between the tall ones. They will form a link to the left end of the arrangement and the low-growing species of plants. From the middle of spring until the end of summer, use liquid fertilizer every two weeks. Make sure the arrangement is kept moist during the winter (see pp. 56/57). Do not cut the plants back until the following spring. The seedheads of the grasses and the trailing shoots of periwinkle will look most decorative throughout the winter. If one of the plants should die during the winter, you may wish to plant pansies or forget-me-nots in the gaps.

Fixing a wall attachment

The usual roof gutter fixtures (obtainable in the building trade) can be used to transform a gutter into a wall garden (see small photograph, p. 40). This attachment can be fixed to the wall with dowels and screws.

Containers

Galvanized metal buckets look good next to a plant container made out of a gutter. The handle of the bucket can be used for suspending it. The best idea is to plant the entire arrangement of plants in a plastic bucket with holes in its base and then insert this into the metal bucket. This will enable excess water to run out of the compost and into the metal bucket which should be emptied daily, if possible, to prevent waterlogging.

Bucket with insert.

Stylish ideas

A romantic flower table

This decorative plant arrangement is perfect for the summer. It has uncomplicated, continuously flowering hanging plants.

Plants for a bowl with a diameter of 60 cm (24 in):
6 busy Lizzies (*Impatiens walleriana*)
4 hanging fuchsias (*Fuchsia* hybrids)
1 large ivy for a hanging container and 3 small ivies with different coloured foliage (*Hedera helix*)
2 *Tradescantia* of different species or varieties

Planting and care
Tradescantia and ivy are available in the gardening trade all year round and at reasonable prices. Busy Lizzie and fuchsias can be bought from the last month of spring onwards. Before planting, make sure that the plant container has drainage holes at the bottom. Cover the bottom of the bowl with a thin layer of compost. Place the green/white *Tradescantia* and the large ivy to the left, hanging over the edge of the bowl and, on the right, plant the other *Tradescantia*. Place the fuchsias and the smaller ivy plants at the front and back between the first two groups of plants. The centre of the bowl should be filled with compost to form a small mound where the busy Lizzies should be planted.
Regularly remove deadheads and leaves. Cut the ivy and *Tradescantia* back if they start to grow all over the flowering plants.
Do not place the bowl directly on the surface of the table. Slip short battens of wood under the bowl so that the drainage holes do not become blocked.

Tradescantia and ivy can be planted individually in containers in the autumn and then used as robust indoor plants even in dark positions within a room.

My tip: Ivy plants are often placed several to a pot by gardeners. You can carefully divide their rootstocks and plant them separately.

Design tip
A certain degree of artistic flair can be achieved with this arrangement if the edge of the bowl is left visible in several places. Once the arrangement is established, the edge of the bowl should be clipped free to expose it in certain places every so often.

Containers
You can create an elegant effect with this kind of arrangement if you use containers with flat edges. You will also achieve a luxuriant overall effect if you choose a terracotta urn as a container.

Securing pots
There are various ways of securing pots to a balcony railing. Decorative baskets and ordinary pots obtained in the gardening trade are ideal for holding replaceable plants or for short-term decoration.
● Bicycle baskets are also suitable for this purpose.

Two decorative wire pot holders.

This cascade of flowers covers everything except the legs of the table.

Successful care

What could be finer than to sit on your balcony or patio contemplating a firework display of colourful flowers high above your head? It can all be achieved by using plants in baskets and hanging containers. To ensure that your efforts are well rewarded and will give pleasure for as long as possible, however, it is worth establishing a regular programme of good care. The advice given in the following pages will help you to do this.

Photo above: Petunias are popular balcony plants.
Photo left: Spray bottle, ceramic cones and watering can are important aids for watering. Liquid fertilizer, fertilizer sticks and granules supply the plants with nutrients.

Successful care

Fertilizing

Plants in containers have to make do with a minimum of compost and are still expected to provide a long-lasting profusion of flowers and vigorous growth. As the nutrients contained in the compost are generally used up after a very short time, you should definitely start fertilizing two to three weeks after planting.

Types of fertilizer

Fertilizer is obtainable in solid and liquid forms, for watering or sprinkling on. It is easy to measure doses of liquid fertilizer into water. Controlled-release fertilizers are also practical. They are offered in granule form to be mixed into the compost or sprinkled on to it later. They will then release nutrients at an even rate over a period of 10-12 weeks. Overfertilizing and the resultant damage to the plants is impossible if controlled-release fertilizer is used properly as, by its very nature, it releases nutrients slowly. The same goes for fertilizer sticks. These should be completely inserted into the compost around the rootstock. The number of sticks to use will depend on the diameter of the container and the number of plants. Fertilizer sticks and controlled-release fertilizer are also ideal if you are combining plants which have varying requirements for nutrients (see p. 30). Use a compound fertilizer for flowering plants. Fertilizer intended for leafy plants, on the other hand, will only encourage the formation of foliage.

Fertilizer for edible plants

If herbs and vegetables are intended only as ornaments, they can be fertilized in the same way as other plants. If, however, they are intended for consumption, the plants should be supplied with nutrients in a different fashion. Growth-promoting fermented herbal brews can be used all summer long. With this form of mild, organic fertilizing, the nitrate content of vegetables and lettuce is much lower than if you use mineral fertilizers. You can also mix a small handful of hoof/horn chips into the compost. Biological fertilizers based on molasses are also obtainable in the gardening trade.

Tips on fertilizing

Please note the following points.
● Continuous rain will wash nutrients out of the compost. This is why plants often look yellowish and unhealthy after sustained periods of rainy weather. Giving them additional doses of fertilizer will usually help them to recover rapidly. Use liquid fertilizer twice weekly, diluted in water and according to the manufacturer's recommended dosage. You can also give the additional benefit of leaf fertilizer. Spray the plants with water containing this fertilizer. The nutrients are then absorbed through the surfaces of the leaves.
NB: Never fertilize plants in full sunlight as this will cause burns on the leaves. The best time is in the evening as the plants will then have time to absorb the fertilizer during the night.
● Dry planting arrangements should be watered with fresh water first and then fertilized, otherwise the roots may suffer burns.
● Granules or water containing fertilizer should not be allowed to come into contact with the leaves (if they do, rinse them off immediately).
● It is better to fertilize plants more often and less plentifully than seldom but in huge doses!
● Plants that are to be overwintered should not be fertilized from the first month of autumn to allow their shoots to ripen before they are moved into their winter quarters.
● You can place liquid fertilizer in a reservoir if the plants are being semi-automatically irrigated (see p. 48).

Spider plants (Chlorophytum comosum) produce long, decorative plantlets. These plants are undemanding but will develop particularly well if they are fertilized regularly during their growth phase.

Watering systems

1 A spray attachment on a pole will help you to water high containers.

To ensure that your hanging garden will thrive and grow vigorously, it will be necessary to water regularly. Both the plants and the hanging containers will lose water through evaporation all the way round and they will require regular and plentiful watering. There are several very different systems of watering that will ensure an adequate and manageable system. You should always make a point of avoiding damage caused by water dripping from hanging containers (see p. 54).

of these materials do not draw water away from plants so the total amount of water given remains available to sustain the plants in their growth.

Watering by hand
(illustrations 1 and 3)

Watering cans: The simplest method is watering with a can with a spray attachment. If the plant containers are hanging up high, you should have taken this into consideration when planning beforehand and have a set of steps handy. These, in turn,

will require additional space for storage.

A spray stick attachment (see illustration 1): This spray-head attachment on a long stiff pipe can be attached to a garden hose. Even containers that have been secured way above your head can be watered comfortably from ground level using this method.

A pump can (see illustration 3): Special watering vessels with a pump attachment for watering hanging containers are now available in the gardening trade. A hand pump conducts water via a pipe up to the hanging container.

Watering plant containers

You can prevent excessive water evaporation through the walls of the containers if you use plastic, stoneware or glazed ceramic containers. Unlike unglazed, porous clay pots, vessels made

2 Ceramic cones and a container of water will replace daily watering for several days.

Semi-automatic watering
(illustration 2)

Irrigation systems that are reasonably priced and easy to install are able to supply water automatically to plants for several days at a time.

Various different types are available in the specialist trade.

Ceramic cones (see illustration 2): Watering is carried out by means of a cone with a thin hose attached to it, the end of which is completely immersed in a container full of water. The cone should be inserted into the compost right to its top. Use two cones for large containers. For boxes of plants, use one at intervals of every 15-20 cm (6-8 in). The surface of the water in the feeder vessel must be lower than the top of the cone. Positioning the reservoir higher or lower will affect the amount of water conducted to the plant container. Light-impermeable material for the reservoir will discourage the formation of algae.

Water reservoirs: Flowerboxes can be obtained with built-in water reservoirs. The compost sucks water up through a wick leading to a tank in the double floor of the container. The reservoir is replenished via a refill pipe.

3 A pump can for very high containers.

Fully automatic irrigation
(illustration 4)

You will hardly need to bother with hand watering at all any more if you install a fully automatic irrigation system. Even long absences will present no problems. The installation is quite involved but the cost and the effort will be rewarded with considerable easing of regular work and an even, superb growth of plants. In these systems water conduction comes from the mains through a valve and an in-built pressure control. The water is distributed through thin plastic hoses. The amount of water and the rhythm of watering is controlled by varying mechanisms. Some systems are even computer-controlled.

Water supply: There are two systems for regulating this.

1 A ceramic "feeler" is inserted into the compost for each irrigation circuit. If the compost begins to lack moisture, the "feeler" emits an electronic impulse that is registered by a valve which opens and provides more water. Once the compost is moist enough, the "feeler" activates the closing of the valve.

2 Regulation via a time clock ensures that water is supplied at regular intervals.

Disadvantage: The supply of water is not controlled by the requirements of the plants and changes in the weather as is the case with a ceramic "feeler".

NB: Check the function of semi-automatic or fully automatic irrigation systems regularly to avoid unpleasant surprises. Occasionally, problems may occur. In all cases, a newly installed system should be closely observed over a certain period of time, just as a trial run.

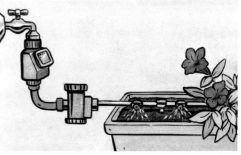

4 Automatic irrigation will care for the plants while you are away from home.

Pests, diseases and mistakes in care

While watering, you should regularly take time to do a thorough check of your plants, especially the leaves and shoot tips, in order to spot trouble as soon as possible. Only quick action can prevent pests and diseases from spreading and endangering neighbouring plants. Mistakes in care can also be the cause of an occurrence of disease and pests. For example, plants that are placed in a position that is not suitable for their requirements, are watered the wrong way or are not receiving sufficient nutrients will all be weakened and this will make them particularly susceptible to disease or attack by pests.

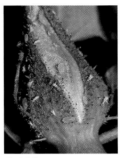

Aphids

Symptoms: Aphids (greenish or brownish-black) suck the sap out of buds, young leaves and shoots, causing sticky, rolled up or crinkled leaves. Ants often follow as they utilise the sticky honeydew produced by the aphids for feeding their young.
Cause: Moist, warm weather and/or weakened plants. If humidity drops again, the aphid attack often subsides. Severe infestation can also occur if plants are overfertilized.
Remedy: Prevention through species-targeted care. Use plant protection agents when plants are infested (see p. 52).

Spider mites

Symptoms: The undersides of leaves are coated in fine web-like structures; light-coloured dots on leaves.

Spider mites.

Cause: Dry, warm, stagnant air and/or weakening of the plant through mistakes in care.
Remedy: Plant protection agents. Prevent with good circulation of air. In advanced stages, web-like structures appear in the leaf axils.

Powdery mildew

Symptoms: A flour-like film on the top and undersides of leaves as well as on stalks and flowerbuds. Withering of leaves in advanced stages.
Cause: Temperature fluctuations as well as constantly wet leaves during cool, wet weather.
Remedy: Do not wet the leaves when watering. Protect the planting arrangement from rain. Prevent by using plant-fortifying agents (see p. 52). Affected parts can be carefully cut off and destroyed. Afterwards, thoroughly cleanse tools and your hands to avoid spreading the fungus.

Sunburn

Symptoms: Reddish-brown or greyish-silver discoloration of the leaves which does not always appear on the whole plant but usually only on the parts of the plant that face the sun. It is easy to confuse the symptoms with those of spider mite infestation.
Cause: Exposure to intense sunlight, ozone burns (particularly on medium-warm days) or frost damage during light night frosts.
Remedy: Prevent through the choice of a position suitable for the species. Newly purchased plants or overwintered plants have to be acclimatized gradually. Protect plants from night frost (see p. 57). There is no protection against ozone damage.

Overfertilizing

Symptoms: Individual parts of shoot tips, buds, flowers or leaves turn brown and start to develop mould. They do not dry up and do not drop off either. The greater part of the plant is not affected by the problem.
Cause: Overfertilizing. In particular, sensitive plants are most affected, for example those with variegated green and white foliage or soft leaves or herbs. Regular doses of fertilizer that are exactly right for nutrient-hungry plants will cause this reaction in more sensitive plants.
Remedy: Immediately cease regular fertilizing. Cut off affected parts.

Dryness

Symptoms: Clearly discernible parts of individual leaves become discoloured yellowish-brown and dry up.

Nutrient deficiency.

Cause: Lack of water in plants that can normally cope with little water (e.g. pelargoniums).
Remedy: Water more frequently. Cut back parts that have become unattractive. Water and fertilize regularly.

Nutrient deficiency

Symptoms: Yellow discoloration of older leaves. The plant becomes bare lower down and looks unhealthy and yellowish. Particularly noticeable after drenching rain showers and in summer plants that grow very fast, like petunias.
Cause: Nutrient deficiency through lack of proper fertilizing, particularly in plants that require lots of food. Heavy rain that washes nutrients out of the soil will also cause symptoms of deficiency.
Remedy: Spray the plant with leaf fertilizer in the evenings or in dull weather (see fertilizing, p. 46). Then fertilize once weekly.

Successful care

Plant protection

Prevention is the best form of plant protection. Avoiding mistakes in care (see pp. 50/51) means that you can eliminate most types of disease. If pests or diseases do appear, check first of all whether the affected plants are provided with the best conditions of growth for their species.

Note the following points.
● Choose the right position.
● Use the right kind of fertilizer and apply the correct dosage. Too much fertilizer can make a plant just as susceptible to disease as nutrient deficiency.
● On hot summer days, water your hanging plants, for example those in baskets, at least twice and do it plentifully, the best times being mornings and evenings. Remember that groups of plants will also dry out on cloudy days with strong winds. Plants placed right up against a house wall or under balconies and overhanging roofs will often not receive any rainwater.
● Water the plants very thoroughly. If the arrangement has dried out, water it several times in succession.

Mechanical methods

The simplest method of preventing infestation by pests is to collect the pests by hand, spray the leaves with a strong stream of water or cut off affected parts of the plant.

Biological measures

A number of biological methods can be used for pests.
● If the infestation is not severe, or even as a preventive, you can use brews, fermented brews or plant extracts. If an infestation has become severe, however, such remedies may not prove satisfactory. Furthermore, they should not be used too often as the plant may become damaged through a reaction to the brews. Plant extracts can be bought in the gardening trade.
● A well-tried home remedy that you can easily prepare yourself is a soap solution mixed with methylated spirits. Insects that eat the leaves or suck the sap of plants, like aphids and spider mites, can often be successfully controlled with this. Dissolve 1 tablespoon of soft soap in

1 litre (1¾ pt) of lukewarm water and add 1 tablespoon of methylated spirits. Spray the colonies of pests with the solution several times at intervals of a few days.
● Garlic brew works well against fungal infections. Crush 1 clove of garlic and pour 1 litre (1¾ pt) of boiling water over it. Allow it to cool, strain and then spray undiluted.
● Preparations that are made out of paraffin or oil. They are non-toxic and do not, therefore, act as a nerve toxin on pests but, instead, clog up their breathing ducts with a film of oil. These preparations should not be used too often or they will also clog up the minute transpiration slits of the plants being treated.
● Pyrethrum extracts are derived from the flowers of an African chrysanthemum. They act as a nerve toxin on pests.
Warning: Although preparations containing pyrethrum are made from plant extracts, they are toxic to humans and animals as well if they enter the bloodstream. Do not use these agents if you have an open wound. Always wear gloves when handling these preparations and never inhale the spray mist. Do not use them in the close vicinity of aviaries, beehives, ponds, rivers or aquariums and keep them away from children and pets.

Chemical agents

These really should be your very last resort when all other methods have failed or an infestation occurs in epidemic proportions. In fact it is often better to replace the affected plants instead of using chemical agents which require so many accompanying precautions.
● Never use highly toxic agents.
● Follow the rules for dosage and use stated on the packaging and also observe the suggested spraying intervals.
● Wear rubber gloves and do not eat, drink or smoke while spraying. Do not inhale the spray mist.
● Only spray on windless days so that the agent cannot drift on to a neighbour's property.
● Never spray in sunlight as this may cause the plants to burn. It is better to spray in the mornings, evenings or when the sky is overcast.
● Always keep plant protection agents in the original packaging. Never, ever store them together with foodstuffs or within reach of children or domestic pets.
● Remains of spray solutions should not be kept as they quickly become ineffective. They should be put into sensitive waste disposal, not poured down the drains (check with your local authority).

Healthy Gazania plant.

Healthy rootstock.

Sick rootstock.

Roots

All plants will develop well if they are watered and fertilized properly according to the requirements of their species. Disturbances in their growth pattern may occur if they receive too much or too little water. In both cases, the plant will wilt and become limp. A quick glance at the root system may help you to determine the cause.

Correct watering: With regular amounts of the right quantity of water for the particular species, a light-coloured, felty root system (see central photo) is a recognizable sign of a healthy plant. The roots are intact and the transportation of water and nutrients from the bottom upwards takes place without any problems.

Incorrect watering: The roots of the plant will become damaged if there is waterlogging or water is provided irregularly. They will first turn brown, then black and begin to rot (see bottom photo). The parts of the plant above the soil will begin to wilt and die because they cannot obtain water. The symptoms are very similar in plants that have suffered either drying out or waterlogging.

Watering and care

A beautifully proportioned hanging garden can transform any area. Throughout the year you can change the look and atmosphere simply through your choice of planting arrangements. However, an arangement that starts off looking beautiful can become a nightmare if the care you give is inadequate or inappropriate.

Plants that are difficult or uncomfortable to reach often end up being neglected so that they are not watered or looked after properly. The result is infestation with pests, disease or, at the very least, lack of proper growth.

The importance of planning

When planning and designing you should ensure that there will be easy access to your hanging garden. This does not mean that you must always keep a tall ladder standing beside a hanging container that is out of easy reach. With the help of easily installed block and tackle equipment or pulleys that can be purchased in a builder's yard, this kind of arrangement can be raised and then lowered to the right height for you to care for the plants comfortably.

Water damage
(illustration 1)

Excess water will simply drip downwards, particularly from hanging baskets.
● Place the arrangement in a position where the water can run away properly and will not damage anything underneath it. The ideal place is above a stone-flagged area with cracks between the individual slabs. On no account should excess water be allowed to run on to a neighbouring balcony or patio.
● When watering, stand a bowl underneath to catch the water running through (see illustration 1). Placing an old cloth inside the bowl will prevent the running water from splashing over the edges.
● Water that runs through should not be allowed to drip on to plants underneath. Such constant showers from above would soon damage them.

2 Complete immersion is a relief for dry plants.

Emergency watering
(illustration 2)

Another way of watering hanging plants is to immerse them. This method is recommended if the compost in the pot has dried out to the point where it will no longer absorb water during ordinary watering.
To do this, lower the hanging container or remove it from its hook and immerse it in a bath of water until no more air bubbles are seen to rise to the surface of the water.

1 Always place a bowl underneath when watering.

When carrying out this procedure, make sure that the shoots do not end up lying in the water or are damaged or made dirty. The best way to avoid this is to hang the shoots carefully over the edge of the bath of water.

Rope and pulley
(illustration 3)

Pulleys are practical aids for lowering large, heavy plant containers. They can be purchased in the building trade, from builders' yards or in ship's chandlers specialising in sailing accessories. They are distinguished by the thickness of the rope and their carrying capacity. Simple or double rope pulleys are ideal for hanging containers or baskets that are not very heavy. Some pulleys are fixed with a screw at the top which means that the entire device can be screwed quite easily into a wooden beam. Others are made for attaching sideways, for example to a housewall. If you use a number of pulleys, you can run the

3 The pulley guides the rope.

rope over quite a distance and in different directions. This makes sense if fixing the rope close to the container is impossible, for example if your garden seat is right beside it. Even if it is conducted across several pulleys, the rope should still move evenly, without sagging. Use a hook firmly fixed in a handy position for tying up the end of the rope. It is possible to buy a kit that comes complete with all essential parts for a practical installation of ropes and pulleys.

Block and tackle
(illustration 4)

In the case of heavy hanging containers, free-hanging balcony boxes (see p. 30) or baskets, you may wish to install a block and tackle between the ceiling and the container (see pp. 16/17). With the help of this device you can lift and lower heavy weights very easily. A reasonably priced block and tackle from a builder's merchant, with a lifting capacity of 200 kg (440 lb) will be quite sufficient for your purposes. Some means

of securing it, in the form of a hook, for example, should be installed in order to fix the rope at the desired height.

Do make sure the apparatus is securely fixed and can lift the weight you propose to hang from it. If you are not a good DIY handy-person, it might be a good idea to have the pulley or block and tackle installed by a professional.

4 A block and tackle make it easy to lower the plants into a comfortable position for you to reach.

Successful care

Caring for your plants

The correct care depends on the requirements of the species of plant. Always check your plants when carrying out daily watering in order to spot pests or diseases in their early stages so that you can immediately take measures against them. Less-involved measures of care, such as removing dead flowerheads, tying up or cutting back, will increase growth and willingness to flower among your plants. Plants are living organisms with a strong urge to grow and survive. With the right care and in the optimal position, they will flower endlessly except during natural, seasonal rest periods or if there has been some kind of growth disturbance.

Deadheading

It is the natural function of plants to produce flowers and, later on, seeds. The formation of seed, however, also brings about the fading and withering of the flower as its natural purpose has now been fulfilled. By regularly removing dead flowerheads, you will prevent the formation of seeds and encourage the production of more flowers. Also, no dead petals will be left to drop down on to other parts of the plant where they will start to decay, thus providing a fertile bed for diseases. If the flower

has a long stalk, remove the stalk along with the dead flowerhead. The trigger for seed formation in many balcony plants often comes in the form of great heat and long periods of drought. In their countries of origin, these plants would only flower during a wet period. Once the dry period begins, flowering ceases.

Cutting back

Dead parts of the plant should be cut off with scissors and destroyed as they can become veritable "nurseries" for diseases of all kinds. Cut back shoots that are too long and also plants that threaten to smother their neighbours or rampage all over the container. Many plants become bushier when they are cut back in a systematic fashion. This is a useful exercise if only one meagre shoot is present. After carrying out plant protection measures, cutting back can encourage plants, that have become weakened through attack by disease or pests, to produce new shoots. A rejuvenating cut encourages flower formation after the first crop of flowers.

Replacing plants

Plants are easy to replace, for example as the flowering season changes, if they are placed in

individual pots. Individual plants that have become unsightly amid a group of hanging plants can be carefully dug out with a trowel. Fresh compost and a new plant can be inserted in the hole. Follow the same procedure for dying plants in baskets. Cut off dead plants in the sides and base of the basket at the neck of the root. These bare patches will soon be covered over by neighbouring plants. You can freshen up the used compost in long-term plant groups if you loosen the surface around the rootstocks and sprinkle fresh compost here.

Overwintering

Outside: Hardy groups of plants can be overwintered outside with a few careful precautions. Remember that, whether full or empty, containers that remain outside must be frost-proof. Ceramic containers will often crack in winter, particularly if the compost in them is moist and begins to expand during freezing weather. Plastic containers should not crack when frozen. They should be kept either in a frost-free room or, if you do not have such a space, under a roofed-over area outside. Cover containers with plants in them with brushwood or something similar and water them on frost-free days. Remove hanging containers and place them in

Begonias and fuchsias will flourish if they are given good care.

suitable winter quarters. Hardy plants removed from baskets should be planted in pots in the autumn.

Overwintering in frost-free conditions: Groups of plants that are expected to be sensitive to cold should be cut back before taking them inside to be overwintered in a position that is as bright and cool (but frost-free)

as possible. A cool conservatory is ideal. Many plants will even flower here during the winter. During the coldest time of year, water them sparingly but do not allow them to dry out.

Protection against early or late frosts

A hanging planting arrangement with plants that are sensitive to frost is easy to protect from light frosts in the spring or autumn if it is moved to a frost-free position overnight or covered over and wrapped up all round in polythene or something similar.

Index

Index

Index

Useful sources

Most garden centres and nurseries can supply catalogues of firms which will supply seeds or unusual plants. The following firms are recommended:

Beth Chatto
White Barn House
Elmstead Market
Colchester
Essex CO7 7DB

**Hillier Nurseries
(Winchester) Ltd**
Ampfield House
Ampfield
Romsey
Hants SO51 9PA

Thompson & Morgan
Poplar Lane
Ipswich Suffolk IP8 3BU
(Will supply a mail-order catalogue and special selections of seeds, seed mixtures for hanging baskets etc.)

Author's note

This volume gives advice on growing and caring for hanging plants on balconies and patios. Some of the plants described here are toxic, can cause skin irritation or may trigger allergies. Very toxic plants, and even less toxic ones that might still cause considerable damage to health in susceptible adults or children, have been marked with a warning symbol in the lists of plants (see pp. 20, 28 and 36).

Please make absolutely sure that children and domestic pets do not eat any parts of these plants. Also make sure that plant containers are firmly secured to avoid accidents and in accordance with your legal responsibilities. Further advice on this matter can be found on pages 15, 16, 17 and 54. Follow the manufacturer's instructions meticulously when using plant protection agents and also note my recommendations on pages 52/53. Store plant protection agents and fertilizers (even organic ones) in a safe place where they will be inaccessible to children and pets. Their consumption can lead to damage to health.

If you receive any wounds while handling soil or compost, it is advisable to consult a doctor to discuss the possibility of having a tetanus vaccination.

Acknowledgements

The author Martin Weimar and the publishers wish to thank Claudia Worner, florist and gardener, for her help in the taking of these photographs. Thanks also go to Angelika Sage, who offered the use of her balcony and patio for photography.

Cover photographs
Front cover: *Gazania hybrids, Dorotheanthus bellidiformis, Portulaca and Convolvulus sabatius.*
Inside front cover: *Pelargonium and Scaevola saligna.*
Back cover: *A comfortable corner in which to sit and dream beneath a basket of begonias and fuchsias (see planting instructions, p. 38).*

Photographic acknowledgements
The photographs in this volume were all taken by Jürgen Stork, except for:
Henseler: p. 50 top right, bottom; Schaefer: p. 51 top left; Weimar: p. 51 top centre left, top centre right, top right, bottom; Zunke: p. 50 top left, top centre

This edition published 1996 by Merehurst Limited
Ferry House, 51-57 Lacy Road, Putney, London SW15 1PR

© 1992 Gräfe und Unzer GmbH, Munich

ISBN 1 85391 598 X

English text copyright © Merehurst Limited 1996
Translated by Astrid Mick
Edited by Lesley Young
Design and typesetting by Paul Cooper Design
Printed in Hong Kong by Wing King Tong

A candlelit dinner on the patio

What could be nicer on a summer's evening than to dine out of doors on a patio where the warm evening air is filled with the enchanting scent of star balm (*Zaluzianskya capensis*) and tobacco plant (*Nicotiana suaveolens*). In this hanging garden these two have been combined with ivy. The best way to grow these plants is from seed during the second month of spring (see sources, p. 60) and then to plant them in hanging containers after the late frosts in the last month of spring. If you wish, you can add *Nicotiana sylvestris* (left in the photograph) which also has a lovely evening fragrance.

An enchanted evening setting with candles and scented plants.

Other titles available in the series

Success with
Fuchsias
Series Editor: LESLEY YOUNG

Success with
Your Garden Pond
Series Editor: LESLEY YOUNG

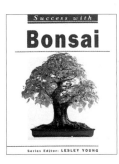
Success with
Bonsai
Series Editor: LESLEY YOUNG

Success with
Hanging Baskets & Containers
Series Editor: LESLEY YOUNG

Success with
Roses
Series Editor: LESLEY YOUNG

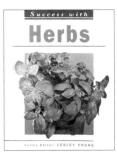
Success with
Herbs
Series Editor: LESLEY YOUNG

Success with
Orchids
Series Editor: LESLEY YOUNG

Success with
Climbing Plants
Series Editor: LESLEY YOUNG

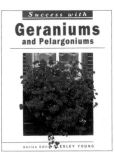
Success with
Geraniums
and Pelargoniums
Series Editor: LESLEY YOUNG

Success with
Camellias
Series Editor: LESLEY YOUNG

Success with
Cacti
Series Editor: LESLEY YOUNG

Success with
Spring Flowers
Series Editor: LESLEY YOUNG